WALKING by FAITH

Kindergarten / Creation

Principal Program Consultants

Rev. Terry M. Odien, MA

Rev. Michael D. Place, STD

Dr. Addie Lorraine Walker, SSND

BROWN-ROA

A Division of Harcourt Brace & Company

Nihil Obstat
Rev. Douglas O. Wathier
Censor Deputatus

Imprimatur
✠ Most Rev. Jerome Hanus, OSB
Archbishop of Dubuque
September 17, 1997
Feast of Saint Robert Bellarmine, Patron of Catechists

The Ad Hoc Committee to Oversee the Use of the Catechism, National Conference of Catholic Bishops, has found this catechetical series to be in conformity with the *Catechism of the Catholic Church.*

The nihil obstat and imprimatur are official declarations that a book or pamphlet is free of doctrinal or moral error. No implication is contained herein that those who granted the nihil obstat and imprimatur agree with the contents, opinions, or statements expressed.

For permission to reprint copyrighted material, grateful acknowledgment is made to the following sources:

American Bible Society: Scripture selections from *THE HOLY BIBLE: Contemporary English Version.* Text copyright © 1995 by American Bible Society.

Confraternity of Christian Doctrine, Washington, D.C.: Scripture selections from *NEW AMERICAN BIBLE.* Text copyright © 1991, 1986, 1970 by the Confraternity of Christian Doctrine. Used by license of the copyright owner. All rights reserved. No part of *NEW AMERICAN BIBLE* may be reproduced, by any means, without permission in writing from the copyright holder.

English Language Liturgical Consultation (ELLC): English translation of the "Lord's Prayer." Text © 1988 by the English Language Liturgical Consultation.

International Committee on English in the Liturgy, Inc. (ICEL): From the English translation of *A Book of Prayers.* Text © 1982 by ICEL. From the English translation of *Book of Blessings.* Text © 1988 by ICEL. All rights reserved.

Cover illustration by Linda Messier

Additional credits and acknowledgments appear on the inside back cover.

Printed in the United States of America

ISBN 0-15-950369-8

10   9   8   7   6   5   4

A Blessing for Beginnings

"So we are always courageous . . .
for we walk by faith. . . ."

—2 Corinthians 5:6–7

Leader: This year we come together to begin our journey of faith.
We are ready to learn from one another and from our Church community. And so we pray:
Dear God, you made everything in our world.
You made us to be your children.
Be with us as we learn and grow.

Reader: Listen to God's message to us:
(Read Isaiah 43:1–5.)
The word of the Lord.

All: Thanks be to God.

Leader: Are you ready to begin?

All: We are!

Leader: Then let us ask God's blessing on our journey this year.
God, our Father, walk with us.
Jesus, Son of God, open our ears to your message and our hearts to your love.
Holy Spirit, help us grow in wisdom and understanding, and keep us in the grace of your friendship.
We ask this in faith, as your children.
May the Lord be with us, now and always.

All: Amen!

WALKING by FAITH

Kindergarten / Creation

To the family of _____:

Dear Family,

You are beginning a wonderful journey of faith.

Throughout this journey you and your child will learn as much from each other as your child does from religion class. This book is meant to help you explore your Catholic faith together.

Each chapter ends with a special take-home activity page. Sharing these activities can be a special time for you and your child. Let your child talk about what he or she has learned. Explore any remaining questions together.

This book also contains take-home Scripture Story booklets. Sharing these stories is a good way to introduce your child to the richness of the Bible.

May God bless you as you walk by faith this year!

CHAPTER 1

A Wonderful World

Prayer

Dear God, thank you for making a
wonderful world.

 God, you created everything,
and you love it all.

Wisdom 11:24

Gifts from God

God gave us our senses to learn about our wonderful world.

smell

taste

hear

see

touch

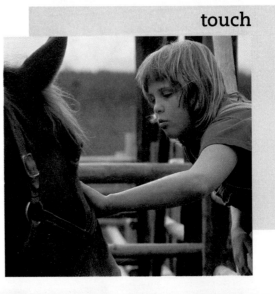

Catholics Believe... that our world shows us God's love.

Catechism, #32

What Do You Like?

Pretend you are at a picnic.

Draw something you like to see, hear, touch, smell, or taste.

Thank God for Our Senses

Color in the button.

Prayer

Thank you, God!

▶ **Family Note:** We've been learning that our five senses help us learn about God's world. Ask your child to tell you how his or her eyes, nose, mouth, ears, and hands help him or her learn about God's creation.

CHAPTER 2

All God's Gifts

Prayer

Thank you, God, for the gifts
that you gave us!

 It is wonderful to be grateful
and to sing your praises!

Psalm 92:1

All Things Come from God

God made everything in the world.

Tell what these children thank God for.

Carlos

Maria

Tyler

Kim

Keisha

Mike

What gifts do you thank God for?

Catholics Believe . . .

that we thank God in prayer.

Catechism, #2637

God's Many Gifts

Draw a special gift from God.

A Thank-You Prayer

Color in the place mat.

Thank you, God.

Prayer

We thank you, God!

▶ **Family Note:** We've been learning about the gifts God gave us. Help your child cut out the place mat. You might work together on similar place mats for all family members. Use the place mats at a family meal. Let your child lead the family in a meal blessing or prayer of thanks.

CHAPTER 3

Caring for God's World

Prayer

God, help us take care of the things you have given us.

 You are my God. Show me what you want me to do.

Psalm 143:10

We Care

Draw how you take care of God's world.

Catholics Believe . . .

we do God's work when we care for God's creation.

Catechism, #307

A Path of Caring
Tell how people take care of God's world.

A Promise to God

Color in the badge.

I ____ promise to take care of God's world.

Prayer

Help us care for all your creation!

▶ **Family Note:** We've been learning about taking care of God's world. At home, give your child an opportunity to cut out and wear this badge while helping you care for a pet, water a plant, and so on.

CHAPTER 4

Mary, Our Mother

Prayer

Mary, our mother, we love you!

Mary is the mother of Jesus.
Mary is our mother, too.

Draw a picture of yourself with
Jesus and Mary.

Catholics Believe . . .

God chose Mary to be Jesus' mother
and our mother, too!

Catechism, #963

A Flower Crown for Mary
Color the picture.

Prayer

Holy Mary, Mother of God, pray for us.

 From now on, all people
will say God has blessed me.

Luke 1:48

Scripture Story

God Made All Things

(Genesis 1:1—2:4)

Family Note: In class your child has learned that God made all things. Read this Scripture Story together. Then have your child use all the pictures to retell the story. Tell your child that you are happy God has created him or her!

And God made people just like you.

Draw yourself.

God made the day.
God said, "Let there be light."

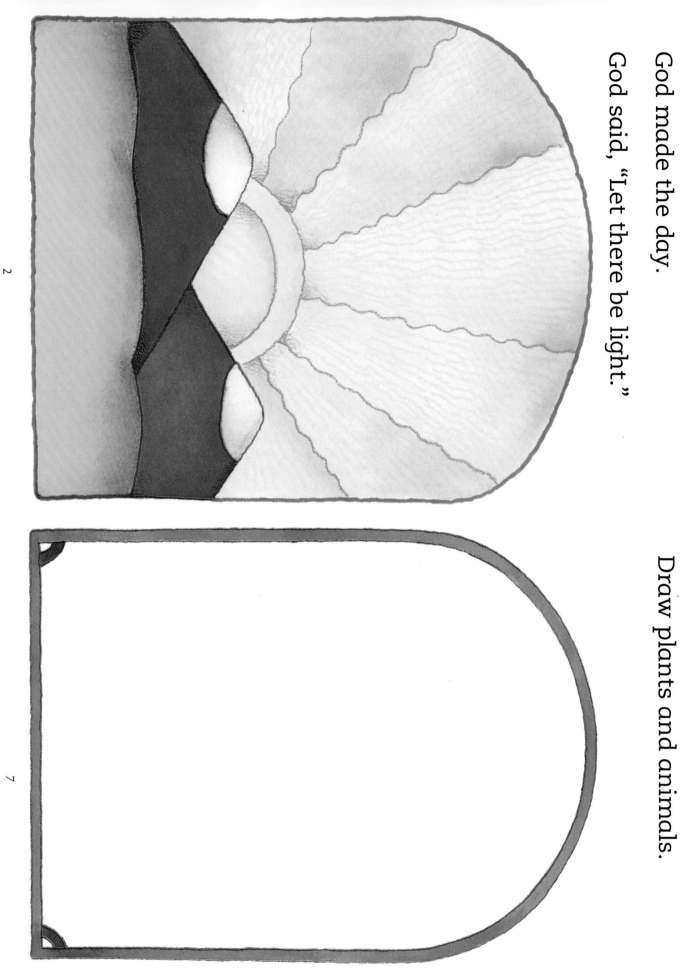

Draw plants and animals.

2

7

Draw the sun.

3

God made the plants.

God made the animals, too.

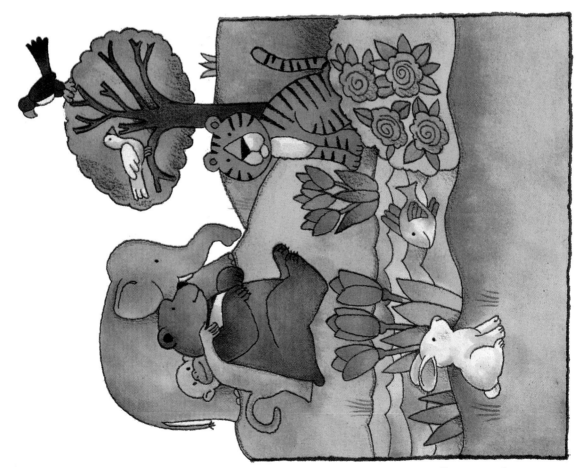

6

God made the night.
God made the moon
and stars so bright.

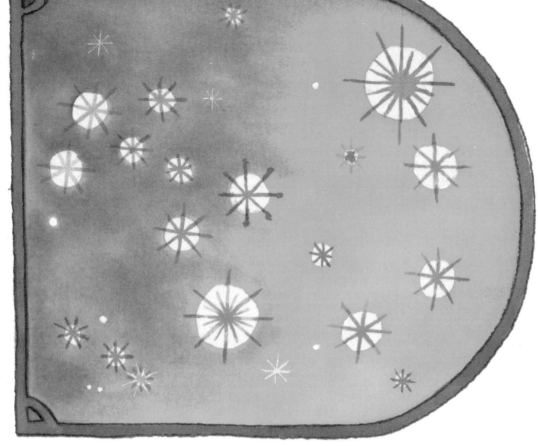

Draw the moon and stars.

4

5

Mary, Mother of Jesus

(Luke 1:26–38)

Family Note: In class your child has been learning about Mary, the mother of Jesus. After reading this Scripture Story together, ask your child to tell you about Mary. Then pray the Hail Mary prayer together.

Pray the prayer to Mary.

Hail, Mary!

Hail, Mary, full of grace,
The Lord is with you!
Blessed are you among women,
and blessed is the fruit
of your womb, Jesus.

8

Long ago there was a girl named Mary.

Mary loved God very much.

2

Color in the name *Jesus*.

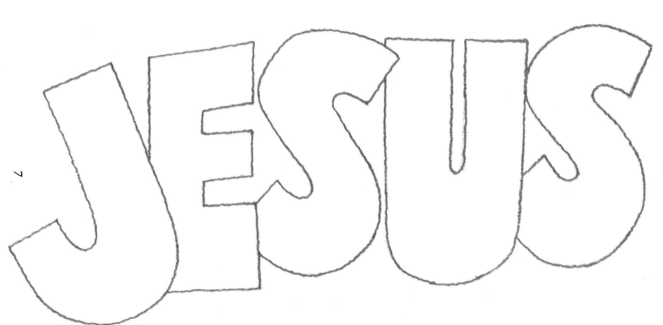

7

Trace the name *Mary* and color in the flowers.

Later on, Mary had a baby boy. She named him Jesus.

6

God sent an angel to Mary.
The angel gave Mary a message
from God.

4

The angel said, "God wants you to be
the mother of his Son.
You will call your baby Jesus."

5

We Love God

Prayer

God, help us know, love, and serve you.

_____

_____

loves God.

God created us, and
we belong to him.

Psalm 100:3

We Share God's Love

Draw pictures of three people you love.

Catholics Believe . . .

that God loves us.

Catechism, #214

We Help Others

Tell how these people help each other.

A Helping Hand

Write the name of someone you will help.

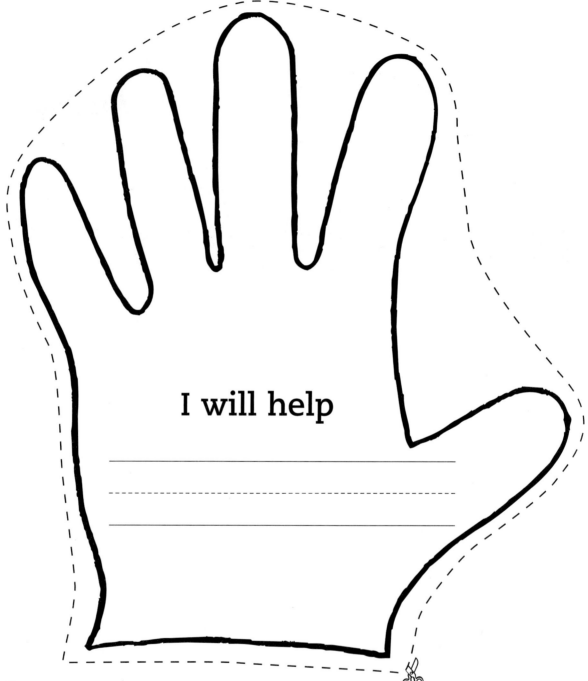

I will help

_____

- -

_____

Prayer

God, we love you!

▶ **Family Note:** We've been learning that one of the ways to share God's love is to help other people. Help your child cut out the helping hand and put it on display. Provide opportunities for your child to help family members and friends.

CHAPTER 6

God Our Father

Prayer

We thank you, God our Father, for your love.

We are all God's children.

 God, you are good to everyone, and
you take care of all your creation.

Psalm 145:9

God Shows Love

How do parents show their love?

by helping

by loving

by forgiving

by teaching

Catholics Believe . . .

that God is a loving parent to us.

Catechism, #239

What Jesus Taught Us

 Color the name for God.

Child of God

Put your picture in this frame.

Child of God

Prayer

Dear God, thank you for making us your children!

▶ **Family Note:** We've been learning that Jesus taught us to call God, "Our Father." Talk about the picture your child has drawn or placed in the frame. Then pray the Lord's Prayer, having your child listen to and repeat a few lines with you.

CHAPTER 7

God Is with Us

Prayer

God, you are always with us.

is with us.

 The Holy Spirit will come
and help you.

John 14:26

The Holy Spirit Helps

Catholics Believe . . .

that the Holy Spirit will be with us forever.

Catechism, #729

God Lives in Us

Draw yourself.

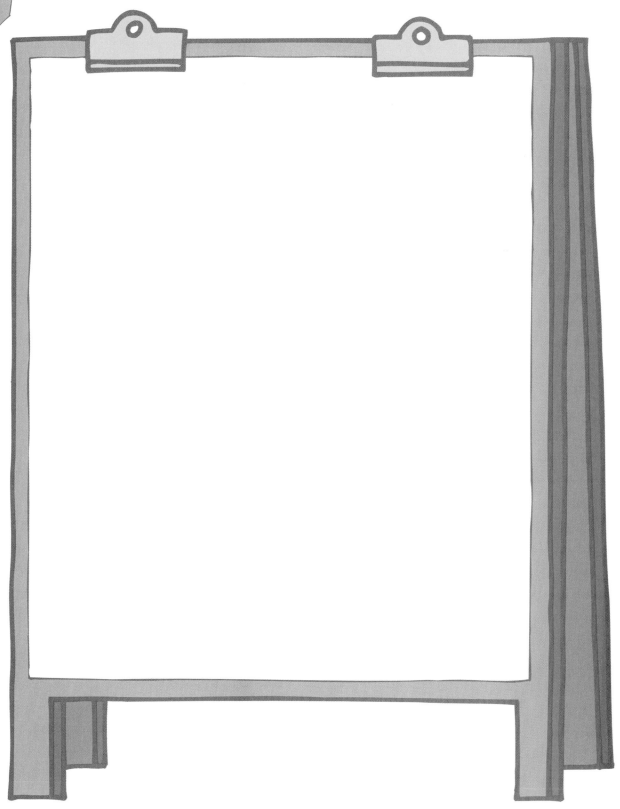

Sign of the Cross

Prayer

In the name of the Father, and of the Son, and of the Holy Spirit. Amen.

▶ **Family Note:** We've been learning about the Father, the Son, and the Holy Spirit. These pictures show your child how to make the Sign of the Cross. Practice making the Sign of the Cross with your child.

CHAPTER 8

All Saints' Day

Prayer

God, help us be like the saints.

Saint Francis

saint

Catholics Believe . . .

that **saints** are God's friends and our helpers.

Catechism, #828

Remember the Saints

Color in the star.

Prayer

All saints, pray for us!

 Everyone who has led others
to please God will shine like the stars.

Daniel 12:3

Scripture Story
Noah's Ark
(Genesis 6—9)

Family Note: In class your child has learned that God is like a loving parent to us. As you read this booklet aloud, have your child use the pictures to follow along. Then have him or her tell you the story of how God helped Noah.

God promised Noah that water would never again flood the whole earth. God said, "A rainbow is a sign of my promise."

Color the rainbow.

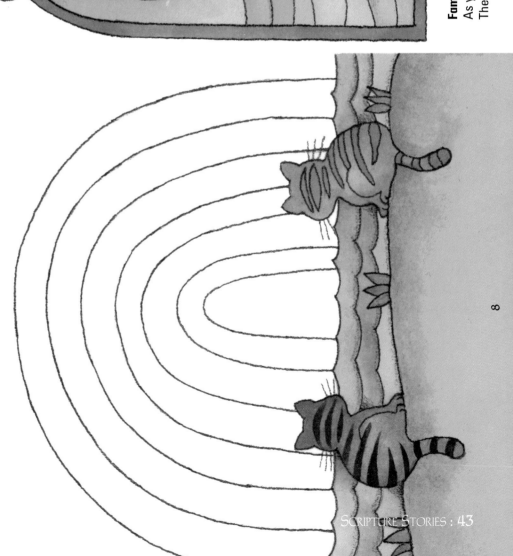

8

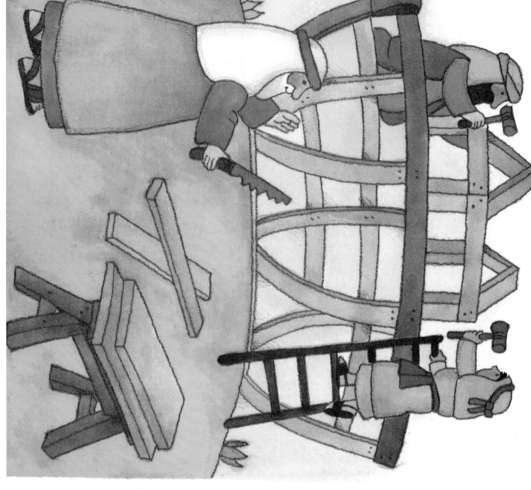

Long, long ago, God told Noah that there would be a flood. "Build a big boat," said God. So Noah built an ark.

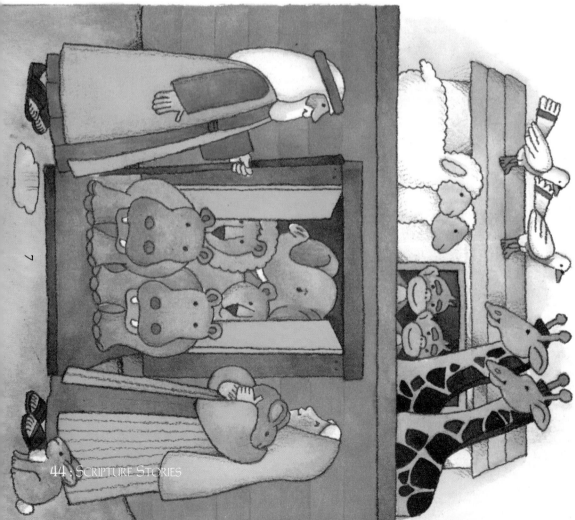

Then the rain stopped. The sun came out. And the water dried up slowly. Noah's family and all the animals left the ark.

7

God said, "Take animals with you, Noah. Get two of every kind."

3

It rained for forty days and forty nights. The water rose higher and higher. Finally, water flooded the whole earth.

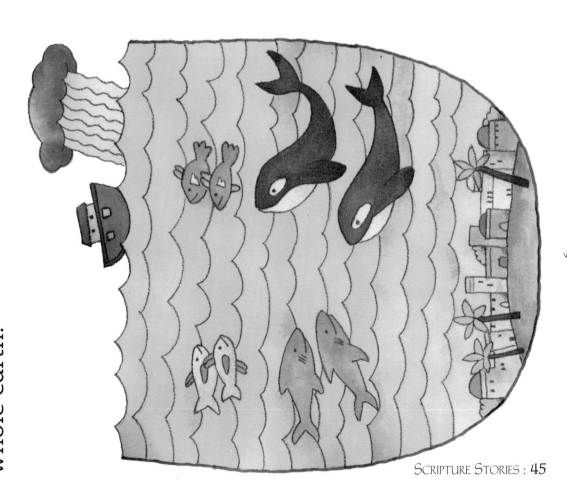

6

Noah led the animals into the ark two by two.

CHAPTER 9

God Sent Jesus

Prayer

Thank you, God our Father, for sending Jesus to us.

 God loved the world so much, he gave us his only Son.

John 3:16

Draw Baby Jesus.

The Bible

Color the cross.

Bible

Catholics Believe . . .

that Jesus came into the world to do God's work.

Catechism, #606

Jesus Shows Love

Jesus fed hungry people.

Jesus healed sick people.

Jesus prayed.

Jesus told stories.

A Bible Bookmark

Color the bookmark.

Name

▶ **Family Note:** We've been learning about Jesus from the Bible, our holy book. If possible, browse through a Bible together and read your child a Bible story.

fold

Prayer

God, thank you for our Bible stories!

CHAPTER 10

The Holy Family

Prayer

God our Father, thank you for the
Holy Family.

 Isn't he the carpenter,
the son of Mary?

Mark 6:3

My Family

Draw your family.

Catholics Believe . . .

that Jesus was a good son.

Catechism, #531

What Families Do

pray

play

work

eat

love

We Are Family
Make a puppet.

fold
forward

fold
back

▶ **Family Note:** We've been learning about the Holy Family. Have your child use the finger puppets along with the stage to tell you about the life of Jesus, Mary, and Joseph. Be sure to tell your child how happy you are to have him or her as part of your family.

Prayer

Holy Family, pray for us!

CHAPTER 11

Follow Jesus

Prayer

Jesus, help us be like you.

Jesus is the Son of God.
Jesus loved God the Father.

Catholics Believe . . .

that Jesus invites us to follow him.

Catechism, #520

Love Your Family

Jesus loved
his family.

 Color the heart red.

I can ⟨heart⟩ my family, too.

 You must love each other,
just as I love you.

John 13:34

Love All People

Jesus loved all people.
I can love all people, too.
Draw how you can help someone.

Be Like Jesus

Write your name.

is like Jesus.

Prayer

Jesus, we love you!

▶ **Family Note:** We've been learning that we were created to be like Jesus. Look at home and in your neighborhood for ways that your child shows loving care and concern for others. Compliment your child for being like Jesus.

CHAPTER 12

Advent

Prayer

God, be with us as we get ready
for Christmas.

 Those who walked in the dark
have seen a bright light.

Isaiah 9:1

An Advent Wreath

Color the candles.

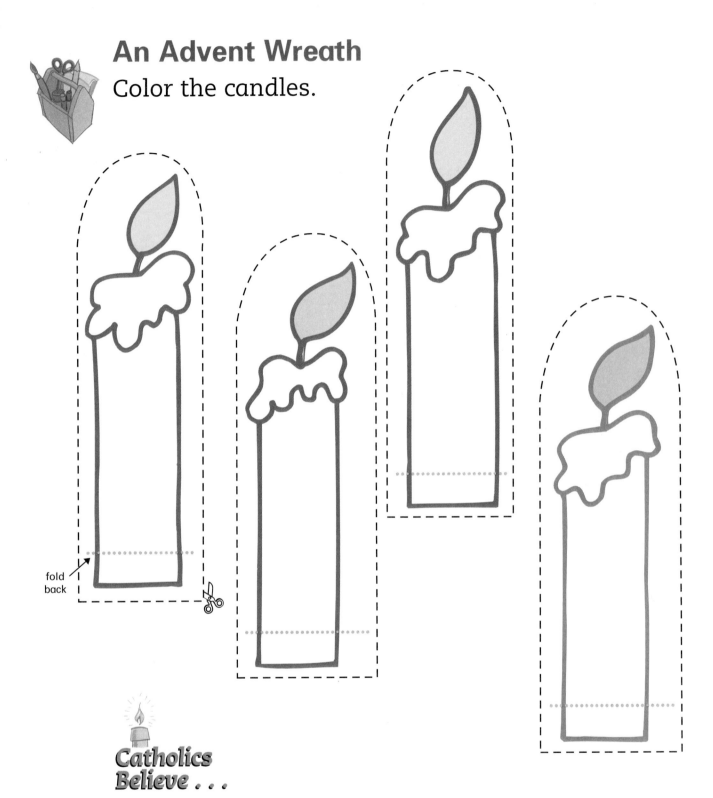

fold
back

Catholics Believe . . .

that Advent helps us prepare for Christmas.

Catechism, #524

Prayer

God, help us prepare for Christmas!

Scripture Story

The Good Neighbor

(Luke 10:25–37)

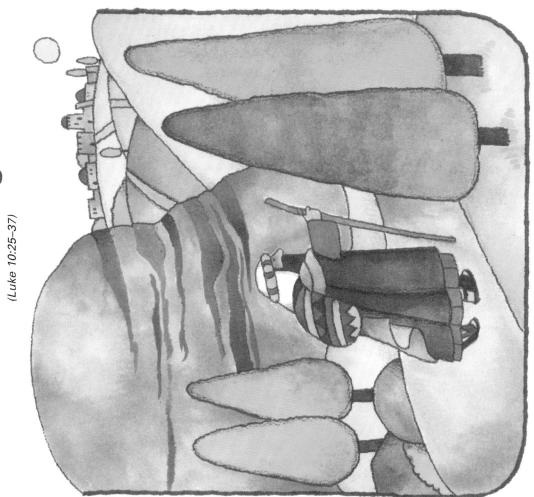

Family Note: In class your child has learned that Jesus taught us to love each other. Read this Scripture Story together. It is the story of the Good Samaritan, a man who loved his neighbor. Ask your child to tell you what the good man did.

Jesus said, "Be like the good man. Love your neighbor."

Color the heart.

Long ago, a man asked Jesus,
"How can I be a good neighbor?"

Finally, a third man came by. He
stopped and helped.
He was a good man.

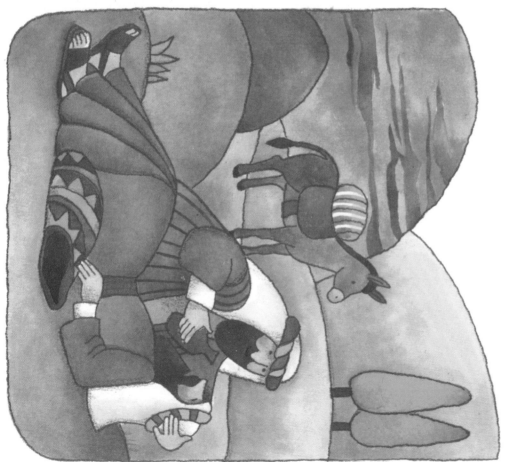

Jesus answered him by telling a story.

Once upon a time, a man was traveling to town.

3

Then, a second man walked by.

He did not stop to help either.

6

All of a sudden, some men robbed the man and beat him up! The man was hurt and needed help.

A little while later, another man walked by. He did not stop to help.

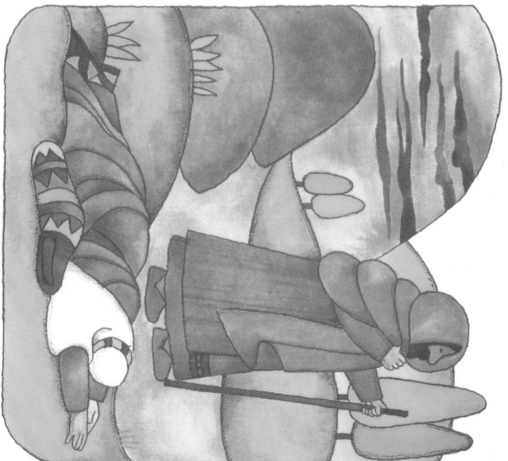

CHAPTER 13

Children of God

Prayer

Dear God, we are glad to be part of your family.

Catholics Believe . . .

that God made people to be part of his family.

Catechism, #759

The Church

 You are citizens with everyone
else who belongs to the family of God.

Ephesians 2:19

God's Family

Draw a picture of people at Mass.

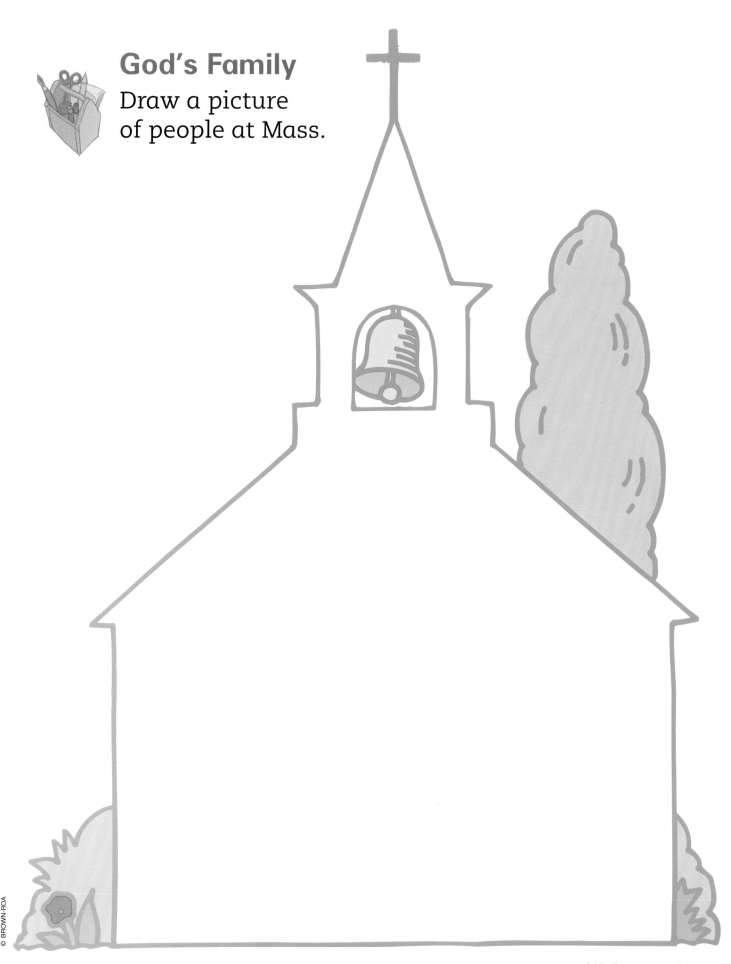

We Welcome You

Prayer

God, thank you for the Church!

▶ **Family Note:** We've been learning that we are all part of God's family. Help your child cut out the welcome sign. Then read the welcome message to your child. Ask him or her how we might welcome new members to the Church.

CHAPTER 14

Our Church Family

Prayer

God, thank you for our Church family.

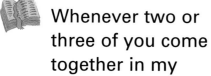 Whenever two or
three of you come
together in my
name, I am there
with you.

Matthew 18:20

Jesus Shows Us

Our Church family follows Jesus.

Jesus showed us how to be good and loving like God.

Catholics Believe . . .

that members of the Church family share God's love with others.

Catechism, #782

The Church Follows Jesus

How does our Church family follow Jesus?

We feed hungry people.

We help people who are sick.

We pray together.

We help take care of creation.

We Share Love

Color the picture.

Prayer

God, help us share our love!

▶ **Family Note:** We've been learning to share God's love. With your child, read the word **love** in the puzzle. Then talk about sharing love as a family at home and within the Church.

CHAPTER 15

Mother of Our Church

Prayer

Blessed Mother Mary, pray for us.

 Mary said, "Do whatever Jesus tells you to do."

John 2:5

Mary Shows Love

good friend

good mother

good cousin

Catholics Believe . . .

that Mary teaches us how to follow Jesus. She teaches us how to show love.

Catechism, #986

Mary Helps Us

Mary helps us show God's love.

Connect the dots.

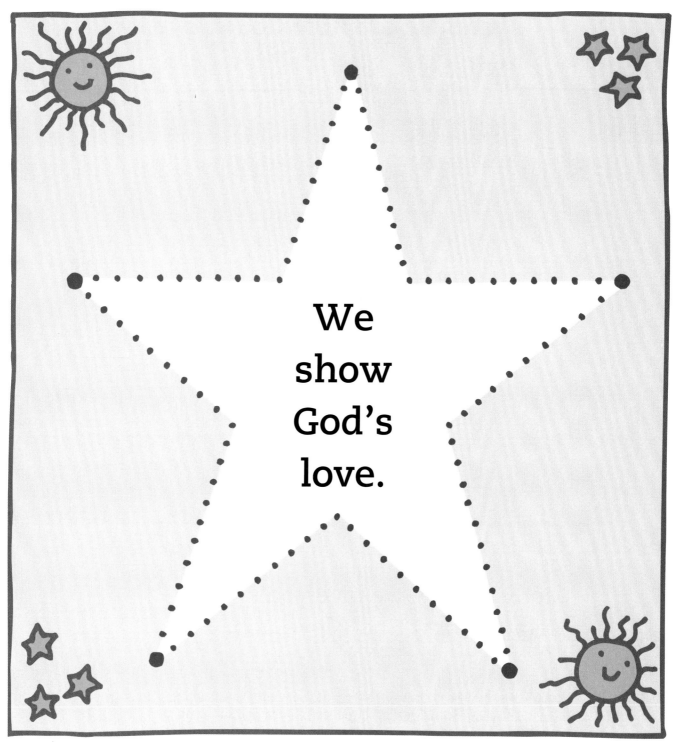

We show God's love.

My Promise

I promise to show God's love.
I will

_____

- - - - - - - - - - - - - - - - - - -

_____

_____

- - - - - - - - - - - - - - - - - - -

_____

_____

- - - - - - - - - - - - - - - - - - -

_____

Prayer

Mother Mary, we love you!
Help us show God's love, too.

▶ **Family Note:** We've been learning that Mary helps all members of the Church family follow Jesus and show God's love. Ask your child how he or she has promised to show God's love. Praise your child for making such a promise.

CHAPTER 16

Christmas

Prayer

God our Father, thank you for giving us Jesus!

Catholics Believe . . .

that Christmas celebrates the gift of Jesus Christ.

Catechism, #526

© BROWN-ROA

A Nativity Scene

Make a nativity scene.

Prayer

God, may there be peace on earth.

Peace on earth
to everyone who
pleases God.

Luke 2:14

fold

Scripture Story
The First Christmas
(Luke 2:1–20 and Matthew 2:1–12)

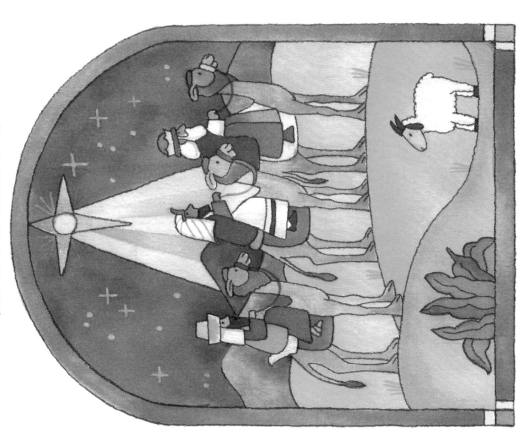

Family Note: In class your child has learned how we celebrate the birth of Jesus. Read this Scripture Story together. Then ask your child what gift he or she would give Baby Jesus and why.

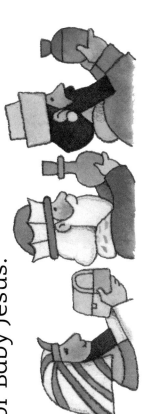

Three kings brought special gifts for Baby Jesus.

What gift would you give Baby Jesus?

Draw a picture.

8

Long ago, Mary and Joseph traveled to a city called Bethlehem.

Shepherds heard about Baby Jesus and went to see him.

They praised God.

When they got there, they had to sleep in a stable.

There was no place else for them to stay!

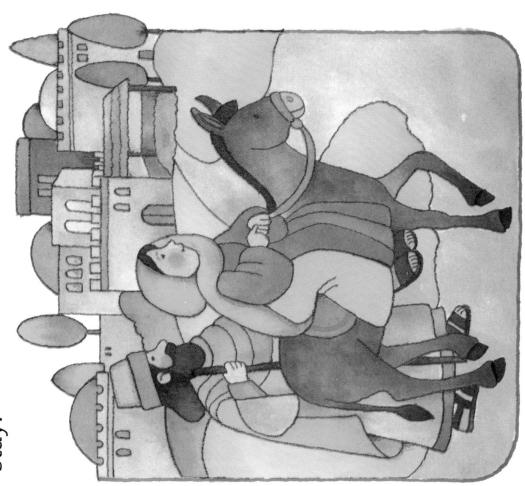

3

A bright star shone over the stable where baby Jesus slept.

Color in the Christmas star.

6

Soon, Baby Jesus was born.
What a special baby!

4

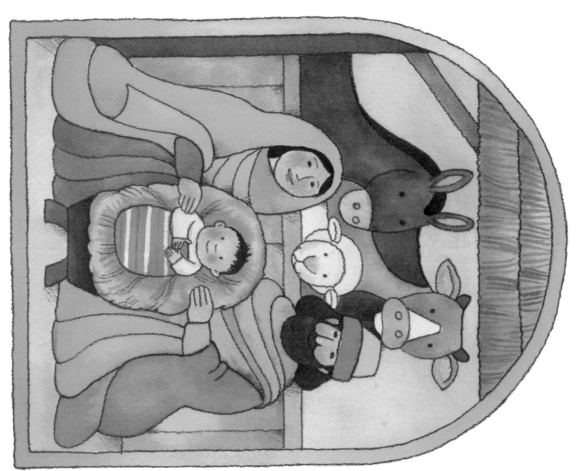

Mary wrapped Baby Jesus in warm
clothes and laid him in a manger.

5

CHAPTER 17

We Are Special

Prayer

Dear God, thank you for making us special!

Catholics Believe . . . that people are God's greatest creation.

Catechism, #357

God Lives in Us
Draw some people.

Treat Others Kindly

 Treat others just as you want
to be treated.

Luke 6:31

Show God's Love

Be kind
to others.

Prayer

Dear God, thank you for all
the people who have been
kind to me. Help me always
be kind to others.

▶ **Family Note:** We've been learning that we show love for God when we treat others kindly. Help your child make a **Be kind to others** poster using this title. After cutting out the title together, glue it onto a large sheet of paper. Then have your child draw or glue pictures of people who are treating each other kindly.

CHAPTER 18

Our Choices

Prayer

Dear God, help us make good choices.

 You will learn what is right.

Proverbs 1:3

Right and Wrong

Some choices are right.

Some choices are wrong.

Catholics Believe . . .

that God helps us choose right instead of wrong.

Catechism, #1954

Making Good Choices

My Helper

Thank

you

for helping me
make good choices.

Prayer

Help us, God, to be strong.
Help us choose what's right, not wrong.

▶ **Family Note:** We've been learning to make good choices. Help your child cut out
the note and present it to someone who has helped him or her make good
choices. You may wish to make other thank-you notes with your child.

CHAPTER 19

Choose Love

Prayer

Dear God, help us make loving choices.

When I hurt someone, I am doing wrong.

 Love should be your guide.

1 Corinthians 14:1

I'm Sorry

Saying "I'm sorry" is a way to choose love.

Connect the pictures.

Catholics Believe . . .

that we show love for God when we make loving choices.

Catechism, #2093

I-Forgive-You Signs

Forgiving others is a way to choose love.

Smile

High-five

Kiss

Hug

We Show Love

Color the flowers.

▶ **Family Note:** We've been learning that saying "I'm sorry" is a way to show love. Talk with your child about the "I'm Sorry" card that he or she has made. Place the card on display. You might want to make a similar "I Forgive You" card with your child. Encourage the entire family to use the cards at the appropriate time.

Prayer

God, I have made some wrong choices.
I'm sorry for hurting others.
Help me choose to love them.

CHAPTER 20

Lent

Prayer

Jesus, help us prepare for Easter.

 Think of farmers who wait patiently
for spring and summer rains
to make their valuable crops grow.

James 5:7

Signs of New Life

Catholics Believe . . .
that Lent prepares us for Easter.

Catechism, #1438

Prayer

Jesus, help us share love.

Joseph and His Brothers

(Genesis 37, 39—45)

Family Note: In class your child has learned that God made us able to choose to do loving things. Read this Scripture Story together. Then ask your child how Joseph showed that he loved his brothers.

They were very surprised to see Joseph again.

Joseph gave them food and said, "I forgive you!"

Joseph still loved his brothers.

8

Once, there was a man who had many sons.

He loved them all. But his favorite son was Joseph.

One year, many of the crops didn't grow.

Joseph's brothers needed food, so they went to see the king's helper.

Joseph's dad gave him a special coat of many colors.

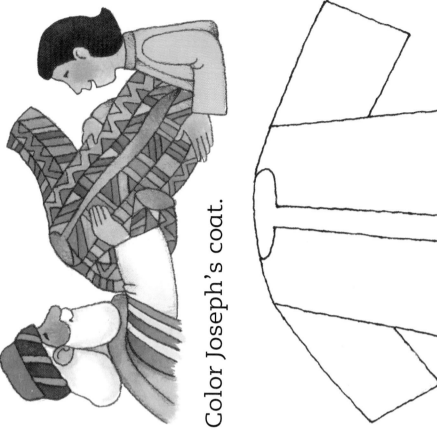

Color Joseph's coat.

3

When Joseph was older, he got a good job working for the king.

Joseph's job was to give food to the people.

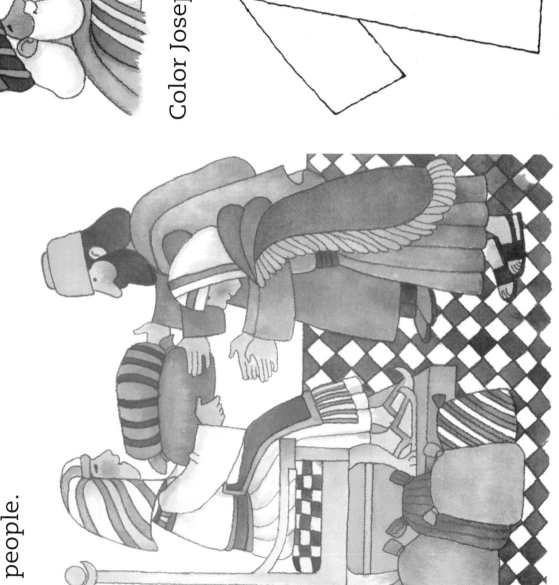

6

The other brothers were angry.
They took Joseph's coat and sent
him far away.

Many years went by.
Joseph had a hard life.

CHAPTER 21

Signs of God's Love

Prayer

Thank you, God, for your love!

 God's saving power is seen everywhere on earth.

Psalm 98:3

Jesus Used Signs

Jesus used signs to help people see God's love.

water

light

Catholics Believe . . .

that water, light, and food are signs of God's love for us.

Catechism, #1147

food

© BROWN-ROA

The Church Uses Signs

The Church uses signs that
show God's love.

water

light

food

My Favorite Sign

What is your favorite sign of God's love?

Draw a picture.

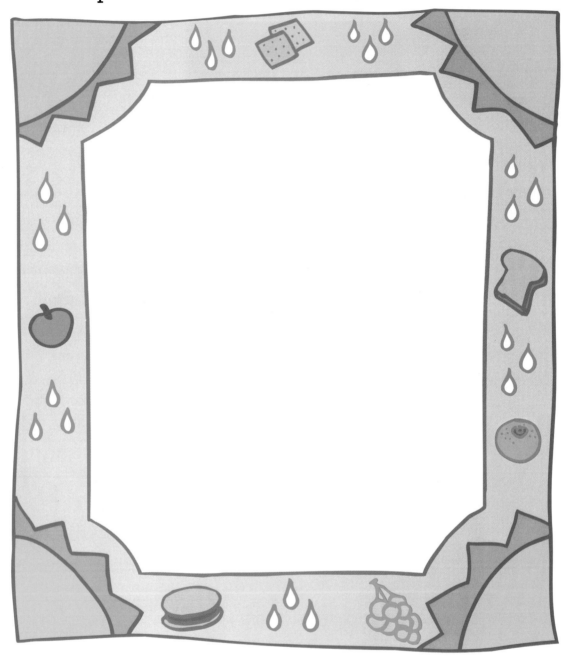

Prayer

Praise the Lord!

▶ **Family Note:** We've been learning that there are many signs of God's love. Ask your child to tell you what sign of God's love he or she has drawn. Remind your child that as a sign of God's love, he or she is very special to you.

CHAPTER 22

God Created Water

Prayer

Thank you, God, for giving us water.

 The water I give is like a flowing fountain
that gives eternal life.

John 4:14

How We Use Water

 **Catholics Believe . . .**
that water is a source of life and also brings new life.

Catechism, #1218

The Water of Baptism

In Baptism the Church welcomes new members.

The water of Baptism is a sign of new life.

Water Brings Life

Find and color all the things
that use water.

Prayer

Thank you, God, for giving us new life.
Help us live as your children.

▶ **Family Note:** We have been learning that water brings life, cleanliness, and refreshment. Have your child tell you why a fish, a turtle, a baby, and a flower need water. Then talk about all the ways in which your family depends on water.

CHAPTER 23

Family Meals

Prayer

Dear God, thank you for the food we eat.

 I am the bread that gives life! No one who comes to me will ever be hungry.

John 6:35

The Last Supper

Jesus ate with his friends.

He shared bread and wine.

Catholics Believe . . .

that bread and wine are signs of God's love.

Catechism, #1333

© BROWN-ROA

Our Church Meal

Jesus shares himself with us at Mass.

The blessed bread and wine are really Jesus.

© BROWN-ROA

We Give God Thanks

The Eucharist is God's family meal.

We give God thanks for love.

Draw yourself at God's family meal.

Prayer

Thank you, God, for bread and wine.
Thank you, God, for giving us Jesus.

▶ **Family Note:** We've been learning that the Eucharist is God's family meal. Tell your child that he or she will be able to receive the Eucharist in a few years. When you take your child to Mass, point out the bread (host) and wine that are signs of God's love.

CHAPTER 24

Holy Week

Prayer

God our Father, help us remember
the life of Jesus.

Catholics Believe . . .
that we are followers
of Jesus.

Catechism, #1344

© BROWN-ROA

We Remember Jesus

During Holy Week
I remember that Jesus

_____

- -

_____

- -

_____

_____

- -

_____

 Christ was humble. He obeyed God
and even died on a cross.

Philippians 2:8

Prayer

Jesus, thank you for living
and dying for us.

Scripture Story
The Last Supper

(Mark 14:1–24)

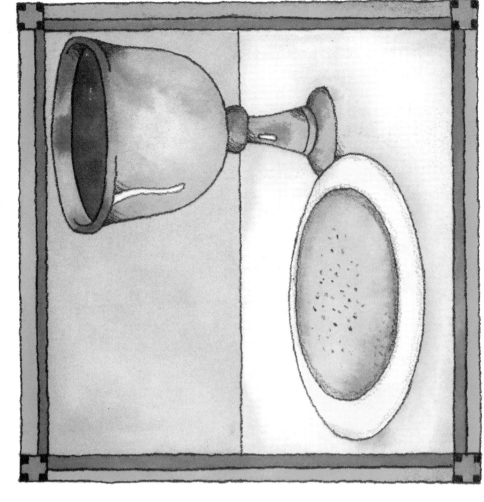

At Mass, the bread and wine become Jesus. We remember him as he asked us to.

SCRIPTURE STORIES : 115

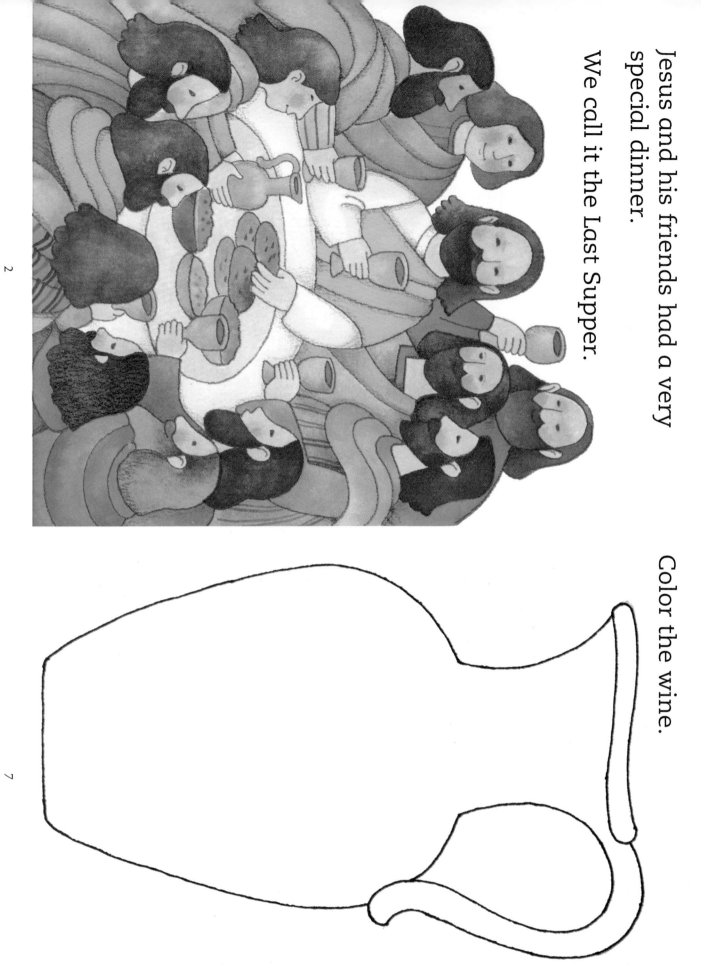

Jesus and his friends had a very special dinner. We call it the Last Supper.

2

Color the wine.

7

This was the last meal Jesus would eat with his friends.

They had bread and wine.

3

Then Jesus passed around wine.

Jesus said, "When you drink this wine, remember me."

6

Jesus passed around bread.
Jesus said, "When you eat this bread, remember me."

Color the bread.

4

5

CHAPTER 25

Heaven Is a Perfect World

Prayer

Be with us, God, when we need help.

rain

heat

snow

wind

What God has planned for people who love him
is more than eyes have seen or ears have heard.

1 Corinthians 2:9

Heaven

Everything is perfect in heaven.

In heaven no one gets sick.

In heaven no one is sad.

In heaven no one gets hurt.

Catholics Believe . . .

that heaven is perfect because God is there.

Catechism, #1024

What Heaven Is Like

Jesus said, "Heaven is like a big house.
God's house has many rooms."
Draw yourself in God's house.

Thank God for Heaven

Find the hidden word.

Prayer

Thank you, God, for heaven and earth!

▶ **Family Note**: We've been learning about heaven, the perfect world that God made. Even though we can't see heaven, we believe it exists. Help your child read the hidden word **Heaven** in the puzzle. Then ask your child to tell you what he or she has learned about heaven in class.

CHAPTER 26

New Life Forever

Prayer

We thank you, God, for the gift of life.

summer

fall

winter

spring

 Jesus said, "Everyone who has faith
in me will live, even if they die."

John 11:25

The Saints in Heaven

The saints follow Jesus.

They live forever with God in heaven.

Catholics Believe . . .

that those who are with God in heaven pray for us.

Catechism, #2683

© BROWN-ROA

New Life in Heaven

Heaven is like a rainbow.

It has many colors and stretches from end to end.

Color the rainbow.

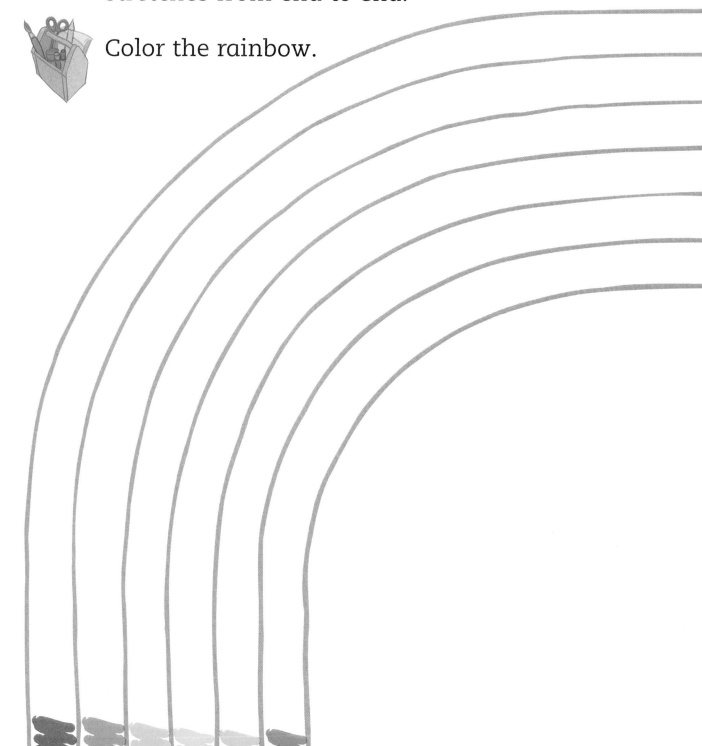

Pray to the Saints

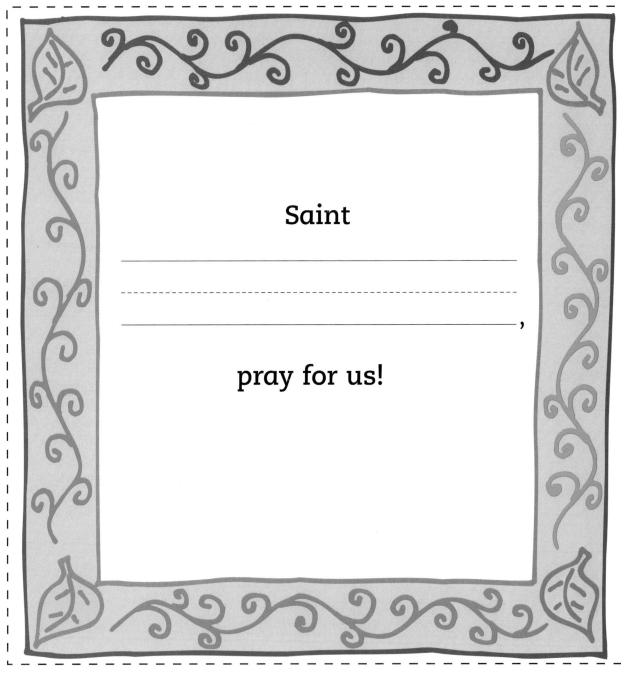

Saint

_____

- - - - - - - - - - - - - - - - - - -

_____,

pray for us!

Prayer

Saints in heaven,
help us on our way to new life!

▶ **Family Note:** We've been learning about the new life God gives us in heaven, a new life that the saints are already enjoying. Help your child cut out the prayer card. Attach the card to a place in the home where your child will see it on display. Encourage your child to pray frequently to the saint for help in following Jesus.

CHAPTER 27

God Makes Us Happy

Prayer

Thank you, God, for fun and laughter.

Your kindness and love
will always be with me.

Psalm 23:6

Why God Made Us

We were made to know, love, and serve God.

We were made to be happy.

know

love

serve

Catholics Believe . . .
that we were created to be happy forever with God.

Catechism, #1721

© BROWN-ROA

What Makes You Happy

Pretend you are on vacation.

Draw something that makes you happy.

Thank God for a Happy Year

Prayer

We love you, God!
Thank you for a happy year.

▶ **Family Note:** We've been learning that God made us to be happy. We are happy whenever we know, love, and serve God. Help your child cut out the smiling face and attach it to his or her clothing. Ask about the happy times your child has experienced both in class and at home this past year. Together, say a short prayer of thanks to God for these happy times.

CHAPTER 28

Happy Easter

Prayer

Dear God, help us celebrate Easter.

Catholics Believe . . .

that Jesus rose from the dead.

Catechism, #638

A New Life

Christ

has risen.

 God set him free from death
and raised him to life.

Acts 2:24

Prayer

**God the Father, thank you for giving
Jesus new life!**

Scripture Story
Easter

(Luke 23:18—24:12)

Family Note: In class your child has learned that Jesus died to save us. After reading this Easter story together, talk about how Jesus rose from the dead, appeared to his friends, and later went to heaven. Then pray the Lord's Prayer together.

Jesus said, "Tell all my friends that my Father has given me new life.

I will come to see you all soon."

On Easter Sunday we celebrate the day that Jesus rose to new life.

Trace the word.

EASTER

SCRIPTURE STORIES : 133

8

Jesus' teachings did not make everyone happy.

Jesus was arrested.

The court said he had to die.

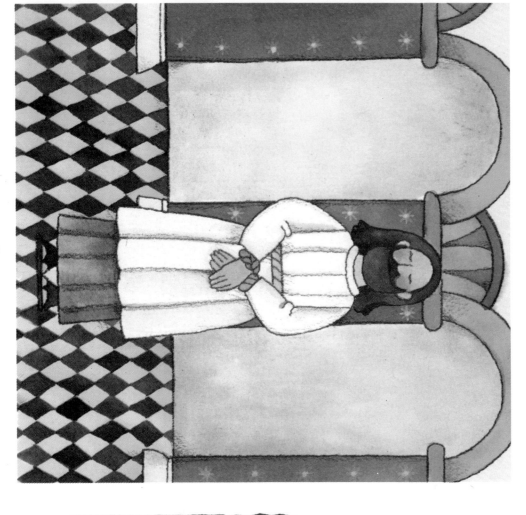

But when Mary Magdalene got to the tomb, the body was gone!

Mary saw someone. At first she thought it was a gardener.

Then she knew it was Jesus!

Mary was happy.

Jesus was forced to carry a very heavy cross.

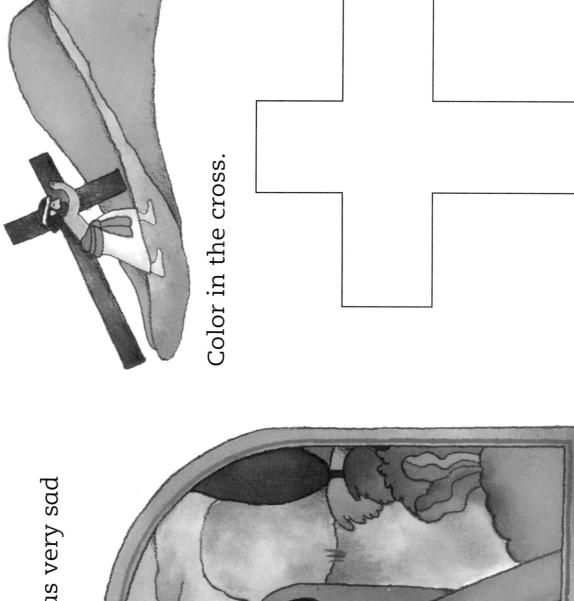

Color in the cross.

3

Three days later, a friend named Mary Magdalene went to the tomb where Jesus lay.

She loved Jesus and was very sad that he had died.

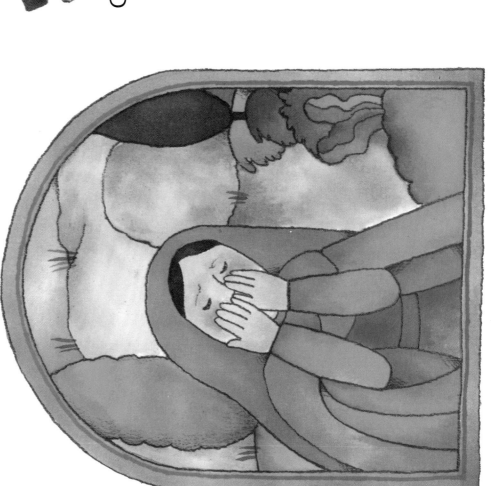

6

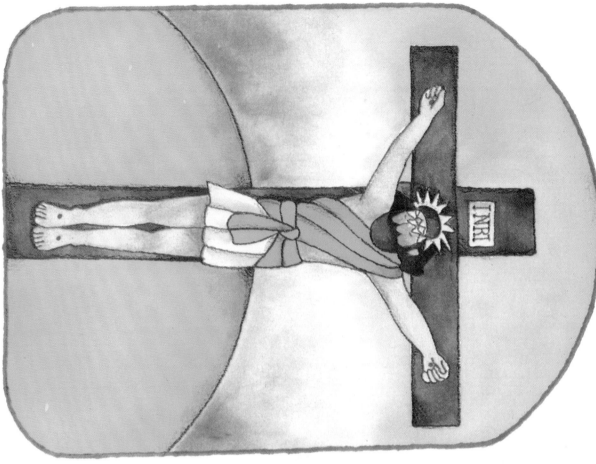

Jesus hung on the cross until he died.

Jesus was buried in a tomb that was cut into a rock.

The Sign of the Cross

In the name of the Father,
and of the Son,
and of the Holy Spirit.
Amen.

The Lord's Prayer

Our Father in heaven,

hallowed be your name;

your kingdom come;

your will be done on earth as it is
in heaven.

Give us this day our daily bread;

and forgive us our trespasses

as we forgive those who trespass
against us;

and lead us not into temptation,

but deliver us from evil.

Amen.

Hail Mary

Hail, Mary, full of grace,

the Lord is with you!

Blessed are you among women,

and blessed is the fruit of your womb,
  Jesus.

Holy Mary, Mother of God,

pray for us sinners,

now and at the hour of our death.

Amen.

Glory to the Father

Glory to the Father,
and to the Son,
and to the Holy Spirit,
as it was in the beginning,
is now, and will be for ever.
Amen.

Act of Faith, Hope, and Love

My God, I believe in you,

I hope in you,

I love you above all things,

with all my mind and heart and strength.

Prayer to the Guardian Angel

Angel sent by God to guide me,

be my light and walk beside me;

be my guardian and protect me;

on the path of life direct me.

Morning Prayer

Almighty God, you have given us
    this day.

Strengthen us with your power

and keep us from sin,

so that whatever we say or think or do

may be in your service

and for the sake of your kingdom.

We ask this through Christ our Lord.

Amen.

Evening Prayer

Lord, watch over us this night.

By your strength, may we rise at
    daybreak

to rejoice in the resurrection of Christ,
    your Son,

who lives and reigns for ever.

Amen.

Blessing Before Meals

Bless us, O Lord,
and these, your gifts,
which we are about to receive
from your goodness,
through Christ, our Lord.
Amen.

Thanksgiving After Meals

We give you thanks for all your gifts,
almighty God,
living and reigning now and for ever.
Amen.

The Great Commandment

"You shall love the Lord your God with all your heart, with all your soul, with all your strength, and with all your mind; and your neighbor as yourself."

—Luke 10:27

The Ten Commandments

1. I am the Lord, your God. You shall not have strange gods before me.
2. You shall not take the name of the Lord, your God, in vain.
3. Remember to keep holy the Lord's day.
4. Honor your father and your mother.
5. You shall not kill.
6. You shall not commit adultery.
7. You shall not steal.
8. You shall not bear false witness against your neighbor.
9. You shall not covet your neighbor's wife.
10. You shall not covet your neighbor's goods.

The Beatitudes

Blessed are the poor in spirit, for theirs is the kingdom of heaven.

Blessed are they who mourn, for they will be comforted.

Blessed are the meek, for they will inherit the land.

Blessed are they who hunger and thirst for righteousness, for they will be satisfied.

Blessed are the merciful, for they will be shown mercy.

Blessed are the clean of heart, for they will see God.

Blessed are the peacemakers, for they will be called children of God.

Blessed are they who are persecuted for the sake of righteousness, for theirs is the kingdom of heaven.

—Matthew 5:3–10

Seven Sacraments

Belonging

Baptism

Confirmation

Eucharist

Healing

Reconciliation

Anointing of the Sick

Serving

Marriage

Holy Orders

A is for angel,
a messenger of God.

B is for Bible,
our holy book.

C is for Church,
our family of faith.

D is for disciples,
followers of Jesus.

E is for Eucharist,
   our holy meal.

F is for forgiveness,
   a sign of God's love.

G is for God,
who made us and loves us.

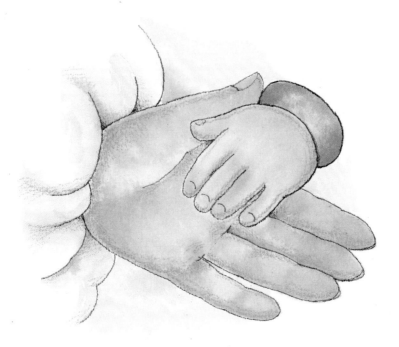

H is for the Holy Trinity,
the one God who is Father, Son,
and Holy Spirit.

I is for initiation, becoming members of the Church.

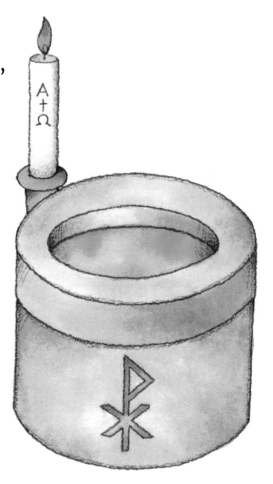

J is for Jesus, God's Son, who saves us.

K is for the kingdom of God:
    justice, love, and
    peace forever.

L is for liturgy,
    when we pray and celebrate together.

M is for Mary,
the mother of Jesus
and our mother, too.

N is for Noah,
who took care of God's creatures.

O is for offering:
  putting ourselves in God's hands.

P is for prayer,
  talking and listening to God.

Q is for the questions
we ask about God's world.

R is for Rosary,
a special prayer to Mary.

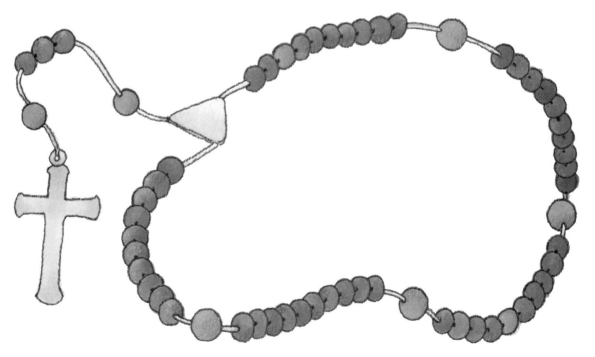

S is for saints,
God's friends who show us how to follow Jesus.

T is for the Ten Commandments,
rules for God's people.

U is for up and down and all around:
God is with us everywhere.

V is for virtues,
good ways to live.

W is for our world,
where all people are God's children.

X looks like a cross,
the sign of Jesus.

Y is for Yes;
we say Yes to God when we say
Amen.

Z is for zebras,
and all the other creatures God
made with love.

INDEX